AF414165

Mastering Real-Time Analytics in Big Data A Comprehensive Guide for Everyone

Lennox Mark

Copyright © [2023]

Title: Mastering Real-Time Analytics in Big Data A Comprehensive Guide for Everyone
Author's: Lennox Mark

All rights reserved. No part of this publication may be reproduced, stored in a retrieval system, or transmitted in any form or by any means, electronic, mechanical, photocopying, recording, or otherwise, without the prior written permission of the publisher or author, except in the case of brief quotations embodied in critical reviews and certain other non-commercial uses permitted by copyright law.

This book was printed and published by [Publisher's: **Lennox Mark**] in [2023]

ISBN:

TABLE OF CONTENT

Chapter 1: Introduction to Real-Time Analytics in Big Data 08

Understanding Big Data and Real-Time Analytics

Benefits of Real-Time Analytics in Big Data

Challenges in Real-Time Analytics

Overview of the Book

Chapter 2: Fundamentals of Big Data and Real-Time Analytics 16

Definition and Characteristics of Big Data

Real-Time Analytics: Concept and Importance

Technologies and Tools for Real-Time Analytics in Big Data

Data Collection and Storage for Real-Time Analytics

4

Chapter 6: Implementing Real-Time Analytics in Big Data

Chapter 8: Real-Time Analytics and Machine Learning   64

Introduction to Machine Learning in Real-Time Analytics

Real-Time Machine Learning Algorithms

Integration of Real-Time Analytics and Machine Learning

Real-Time Anomaly Detection using Machine Learning

Chapter 9: Security and Privacy in Real-Time Analytics   72

Challenges and Risks in Real-Time Analytics Security

Data Privacy and Compliance Considerations

Real-Time Threat Detection and Mitigation

Best Practices for Securing Real-Time Analytics Systems

Chapter 10: Future Trends and Innovations in Real-Time Analytics   81

Edge Computing and Real-Time Analytics

Artificial Intelligence and Real-Time Analytics

Internet of Things (IoT) and Real-Time Analytics

Predictive Analytics and Real-Time Decision-Making

Chapter 1: Introduction to Real-Time Analytics in Big Data

Understanding Big Data and Real-Time Analytics

In today's digital age, data is being generated at an unprecedented rate. Every day, we create 2.5 quintillion bytes of data, and this number is expected to increase exponentially in the coming years. This explosion of data has given rise to the concept of Big Data Analytics, which involves extracting useful insights from massive datasets. In this subchapter, we will delve into the world of Big Data and explore the fascinating field of real-time analytics.

Big Data refers to extremely large and complex datasets that cannot be effectively processed using traditional data processing techniques. It encompasses structured, semi-structured, and unstructured data from various sources, including social media, sensors, and transactional systems. The immense volume, velocity, and variety of Big Data pose significant challenges in terms of storage, processing, and analysis.

Real-time analytics, on the other hand, is the practice of analyzing data as it is generated, enabling organizations to make immediate, data-driven decisions. Real-time analytics leverages advanced technologies such as machine learning, artificial intelligence, and predictive modeling to extract valuable insights from streaming data. By analyzing data in real-time, organizations can detect anomalies, identify trends, and respond quickly to changing market conditions.

The combination of Big Data and real-time analytics offers numerous benefits across industries. For instance, in healthcare, real-time analytics can help monitor patient vitals in real-time, enabling doctors to detect any abnormalities and provide timely interventions. In finance, real-time analytics can detect fraudulent transactions and trigger immediate alerts to prevent financial losses. In retail, real-time analytics can provide personalized recommendations to customers based on their browsing and purchase history.

To effectively harness the power of Big Data and real-time analytics, organizations need robust infrastructure and advanced analytics tools. This includes distributed storage systems like Hadoop, which can handle large volumes of data, and stream processing frameworks like Apache Kafka, which can ingest and process real-time data streams. Additionally, organizations need skilled data scientists and analysts who can interpret the results and translate them into actionable insights.

In conclusion, Big Data and real-time analytics have revolutionized the way organizations operate and make decisions. By understanding the intricacies of Big Data and leveraging real-time analytics, businesses can gain a competitive edge in today's data-driven world. This subchapter serves as a comprehensive guide for everyone interested in the field of Big Data Analytics, providing insights into the fundamentals and the potential applications of real-time analytics. Whether you are a business professional, a data scientist, or simply curious about the power of data, this subchapter will equip you with the knowledge and tools to navigate the world of Big Data and real-time analytics.

Benefits of Real-Time Analytics in Big Data

Real-time analytics in big data has revolutionized the way businesses operate, enabling them to make informed decisions and gain a competitive edge in today's data-driven world. This subchapter will explore the numerous benefits that real-time analytics brings to the field of big data analytics, and why it is essential for everyone, regardless of their industry or profession, to understand and leverage this powerful tool.

One of the most significant advantages of real-time analytics is the ability to make instant decisions based on up-to-date information. Traditional analytics methods often rely on historical data, which may not accurately reflect the current market conditions or customer behavior. With real-time analytics, businesses can access and analyze data as it is generated, allowing them to respond promptly to market changes, identify trends, and seize opportunities before their competitors.

Real-time analytics also enhances data visibility and transparency. By continuously monitoring and analyzing data in real-time, businesses gain a comprehensive understanding of their operations, customer behavior, and market dynamics. This visibility enables organizations to identify bottlenecks, inefficiencies, and areas for improvement, leading to optimized processes and increased operational efficiency.

Another significant benefit of real-time analytics in big data is its impact on customer experience. By analyzing customer data in real-time, businesses can personalize their offerings, tailor marketing campaigns, and deliver targeted advertisements based on individual preferences and behaviors. This level of personalization not only improves customer satisfaction but also drives customer loyalty and increases revenue.

Real-time analytics also plays a crucial role in fraud detection and cybersecurity. By continuously monitoring data streams, businesses can detect anomalies and patterns that indicate potential security breaches or fraudulent activities. With real-time analytics, organizations can respond swiftly to mitigate risks, protect sensitive information, and prevent financial losses.

Additionally, real-time analytics enables predictive analytics, which helps businesses anticipate future trends and make proactive decisions. By analyzing real-time data alongside historical data, organizations can identify patterns, predict customer behavior, and forecast market trends with greater accuracy. These predictive insights empower businesses to optimize their strategies, allocate resources effectively, and stay ahead of the competition.

In conclusion, real-time analytics in big data offers numerous benefits across various industries and professions. From making informed, data-driven decisions to enhancing customer experience and optimizing operations, real-time analytics has become an indispensable tool for businesses worldwide. By embracing and mastering real-time analytics, individuals and organizations can unlock the full potential of big data analytics and gain a competitive advantage in today's data-driven landscape.

Challenges in Real-Time Analytics

Real-time analytics has emerged as a powerful tool in the field of big data analytics, enabling organizations to make informed decisions and take immediate actions based on up-to-the-minute data insights. However, this cutting-edge technology is not without its challenges. In this subchapter, we will explore some of the key hurdles faced by organizations when implementing real-time analytics in the context of big data.

One of the primary challenges in real-time analytics is the sheer volume and velocity of data. With the proliferation of connected devices and the increasing digitization of processes, organizations are inundated with massive amounts of data that need to be processed and analyzed in real-time. This requires robust infrastructure and high-performance systems capable of handling the data deluge.

Another significant challenge is ensuring data quality and accuracy. Real-time analytics heavily relies on the accuracy and integrity of the data being analyzed. However, with data coming from various sources and in different formats, ensuring data quality becomes a complex task. Organizations must invest in data cleansing, normalization, and validation processes to ensure accurate insights and reliable decision-making.

Furthermore, real-time analytics often requires complex event processing (CEP) capabilities to identify patterns, anomalies, and trends in real-time data streams. Implementing CEP systems and algorithms can be a daunting task, requiring specialized skills and expertise. Organizations must invest in training their personnel or hire data scientists who can develop and deploy these advanced analytical models effectively.

In addition to technical challenges, there are also organizational and cultural hurdles. Many organizations struggle with integrating real-time analytics into their existing workflows and decision-making processes. This often requires a shift in mindset and a cultural transformation to embrace data-driven decision-making. Leadership support and clear communication are crucial to overcoming these challenges and ensuring successful adoption of real-time analytics.

Lastly, data privacy and security pose significant challenges in real-time analytics. As data is analyzed and processed in real-time, organizations need to ensure that sensitive information is protected and comply with data privacy regulations. Implementing robust security measures and encryption protocols becomes imperative to safeguard data integrity and protect customer privacy.

In conclusion, while real-time analytics offers immense potential for organizations to gain actionable insights from big data, it also presents several challenges. Overcoming these challenges requires a combination of technical expertise, organizational readiness, and a commitment to data-driven decision-making. By addressing these challenges head-on, organizations can unlock the full potential of real-time analytics to drive innovation, improve operational efficiency, and gain a competitive edge in the era of big data.

Overview of the Book

In today's data-driven world, harnessing the power of big data analytics has become crucial for organizations of all sizes and industries. The book "Mastering Real-Time Analytics in Big Data: A Comprehensive Guide for Everyone" aims to provide a comprehensive overview and practical insights into the world of big data analytics.

Addressed to a wide audience of "EVERY ONE," this book is designed to cater to individuals from various backgrounds, ranging from data scientists and engineers to business executives and decision-makers. Whether you are a seasoned professional or a newcomer to the field of big data analytics, this book offers something for everyone.

The first section of the book delves into the fundamentals of big data analytics, explaining what it is and why it matters. It covers the underlying technologies and architectures used to process and analyze massive amounts of data in real-time. The authors take a no-nonsense approach, making complex concepts accessible to readers from all niches of the big data analytics world.

The subsequent chapters walk readers through the entire process of building a real-time analytics pipeline. From data ingestion and storage to processing and visualization, each step is explained in detail, accompanied by practical examples and case studies. The authors emphasize the importance of selecting the right tools and technologies, providing recommendations and best practices for implementation.

Furthermore, the book explores various advanced topics in big data analytics, such as machine learning, artificial intelligence, and predictive analytics. It highlights the potential of these technologies to unlock valuable insights and drive business outcomes. Real-world examples and use cases demonstrate how organizations have successfully leveraged these techniques to gain a competitive edge in today's data-driven marketplace.

Throughout the book, the authors emphasize the importance of data privacy, ethics, and security. They provide guidance on safeguarding sensitive information and complying with relevant regulations. Additionally, they discuss the challenges and potential pitfalls in real-time analytics and offer strategies to overcome them.

"Mastering Real-Time Analytics in Big Data: A Comprehensive Guide for Everyone" is not just another technical manual. It is a holistic guide that empowers individuals from all backgrounds to understand and harness the power of big data analytics. Whether you are a professional seeking to enhance your skills or a business leader exploring new opportunities, this book will equip you with the knowledge and insights needed to thrive in the world of big data analytics.

Chapter 2: Fundamentals of Big Data and Real-Time Analytics

Definition and Characteristics of Big Data

In today's data-driven world, the term "big data" has become ubiquitous. It refers to the massive amount of structured, semi-structured, and unstructured data that is generated from various sources at an unprecedented velocity. This data is too vast and complex to be effectively managed and analyzed using traditional data processing techniques. As a result, big data analytics has emerged as a crucial field, enabling organizations to extract valuable insights and make informed decisions.

Big data is characterized by three primary attributes, commonly known as the three Vs: volume, velocity, and variety. These characteristics differentiate big data from traditional datasets and pose unique challenges for its storage, processing, and analysis.

Volume refers to the vast amount of data being generated every second. With the proliferation of digital devices, social media platforms, and the Internet of Things (IoT), the volume of data has skyrocketed. Organizations now have access to massive datasets, often in the terabytes or petabytes range. Handling this enormous volume requires specialized tools and technologies capable of storing and processing such data efficiently.

Velocity represents the speed at which data is generated and needs to be processed in real-time. Big data analytics focuses on extracting insights from data in real-time or near-real-time, allowing organizations to respond quickly to changing market dynamics. To achieve real-time analytics, organizations must leverage technologies that can process data streams rapidly and provide instant results.

Variety refers to the diverse types and formats of data that big data encompasses. Traditional data sources typically consist of structured data, such as relational databases. However, big data includes semi-structured and unstructured data as well, such as emails, social media posts, images, videos, and sensor data. Analyzing this diverse range of data sources requires advanced techniques, including natural language processing, image recognition, and sentiment analysis.

Furthermore, big data is often characterized by two additional Vs: veracity and value. Veracity refers to the quality and reliability of the data. Due to its sheer volume and variety, big data can be noisy and contain inconsistencies, errors, or biases. Ensuring data quality is crucial for accurate analysis and reliable insights. Value represents the importance and relevance of the data. Organizations must identify the data that holds value and align it with their business objectives to derive meaningful insights and drive decision-making.

Understanding the definition and characteristics of big data is fundamental for anyone interested in the field of big data analytics. With the right tools, technologies, and methodologies, organizations can harness the power of big data and unlock invaluable insights that can lead to improved business strategies, enhanced operational efficiency, and competitive advantage in today's data-driven landscape.

Real-Time Analytics: Concept and Importance

In today's era of Big Data analytics, the ability to extract valuable insights from massive amounts of data in real-time has become crucial for businesses of all sizes and across various industries. Real-time analytics refers to the process of analyzing data as it is generated or received, allowing organizations to make informed and timely decisions.

Real-time analytics leverages advanced technologies and algorithms to process data in real-time, enabling businesses to gain instant insights into customer behavior, market trends, operational efficiency, and more. It involves the collection, integration, and analysis of streaming data from multiple sources, including IoT devices, social media platforms, transactional systems, and sensor networks.

One of the key benefits of real-time analytics is its ability to provide businesses with a competitive edge. By analyzing data in real-time, organizations can quickly identify patterns, trends, and anomalies, allowing them to respond promptly to changing market conditions. This agility enables businesses to optimize their operations, improve customer engagement, and increase revenue.

Real-time analytics also plays a vital role in enhancing customer experience. By analyzing customer data in real-time, organizations can personalize their offerings, provide targeted recommendations, and deliver real-time customer support. This level of personalization not only leads to increased customer satisfaction but also fosters customer loyalty and retention.

Another significant application of real-time analytics is in fraud detection and prevention. By continuously monitoring transactional data in real-time, organizations can identify suspicious activities and take immediate action to prevent fraud. This proactive approach helps businesses save significant financial losses and safeguards their reputation.

Furthermore, real-time analytics contributes to operational efficiency by enabling organizations to monitor and optimize their processes in real-time. It allows businesses to identify bottlenecks, streamline operations, and make data-driven decisions that lead to cost reductions and improved productivity.

In conclusion, real-time analytics is a critical concept in the field of Big Data analytics. Its importance lies in its ability to provide businesses with real-time insights, enabling them to make informed decisions, improve customer experience, detect fraud, and enhance operational efficiency. By embracing real-time analytics, organizations can harness the power of Big Data and gain a competitive advantage in today's data-driven world.

Technologies and Tools for Real-Time Analytics in Big Data

In today's data-driven world, big data analytics has become an integral part of businesses across various industries. The ability to analyze and gain insights from vast amounts of data in real-time is crucial for making informed decisions, identifying trends, and gaining a competitive edge. This subchapter explores the technologies and tools that enable real-time analytics in the realm of big data, making it a comprehensive guide for everyone interested in the niche of big data analytics.

Apache Hadoop is one of the most widely used technologies for big data analytics. It provides a distributed file system and a framework for processing and analyzing large datasets across clusters of computers. Hadoop's MapReduce algorithm allows for parallel processing and scalability, making it ideal for handling massive amounts of data. Additionally, Hadoop's ecosystem includes various tools such as Apache Spark, Hive, and Pig, which provide additional functionalities for real-time analytics.

Apache Kafka is another essential technology for real-time analytics in big data. It is a distributed streaming platform that allows for the collection, processing, and analysis of data streams in real-time. Kafka provides high scalability, fault tolerance, and low-latency data processing, making it well-suited for use cases that require real-time analytics, such as fraud detection, social media sentiment analysis, and IoT data processing.

In-memory databases, such as Apache Ignite and Apache Spark, play a vital role in real-time analytics. These databases store data in the main memory, enabling faster data access and processing compared to traditional disk-based databases. In-memory databases are particularly useful for applications that require real-time querying and analysis of large datasets.

Real-time analytics also heavily relies on stream processing frameworks like Apache Flink and Apache Storm. These frameworks enable the processing and analysis of continuous data streams in real-time, allowing businesses to respond and act on insights immediately. Stream processing frameworks are widely used in applications like clickstream analysis, stock market analysis, and network monitoring.

Furthermore, cloud-based platforms like Amazon Web Services (AWS), Google Cloud Platform (GCP), and Microsoft Azure offer a range of services and tools for real-time analytics in big data. These platforms provide scalable storage, processing, and analysis capabilities, allowing businesses to leverage the power of the cloud for real-time analytics without the need for heavy investments in infrastructure.

In conclusion, the technologies and tools discussed in this subchapter are essential for mastering real-time analytics in big data. Whether you are a business professional, data scientist, or technology enthusiast, understanding and leveraging these tools can help you unlock the full potential of big data analytics and gain valuable insights in real-time.

Data Collection and Storage for Real-Time Analytics

In today's age of digital transformation and ever-increasing data volumes, real-time analytics has become crucial for businesses across all industries. The ability to process and analyze data in real-time enables organizations to make informed decisions, identify patterns, and gain valuable insights that can drive growth and innovation. However, to achieve effective real-time analytics, proper data collection and storage mechanisms are essential.

Data collection forms the foundation of any analytics initiative. It involves gathering relevant data from various sources, such as customer interactions, social media, sensor networks, and transaction logs. The data collected can be structured, semi-structured, or unstructured, and may come in different formats, including text, images, audio, and video. It is important to employ robust data collection techniques that ensure accuracy, completeness, and timeliness.

Real-time analytics heavily relies on data streaming, where data is continuously generated and processed in real-time. To facilitate this, organizations must adopt modern data collection technologies that can handle high volumes of data and provide low-latency processing. These technologies include event-driven architectures, message queuing systems, and stream processing frameworks like Apache Kafka and Apache Flink.

Once the data is collected, it needs to be stored in a manner that allows quick and efficient retrieval. Traditional data storage systems, such as relational databases, may not be suitable for real-time analytics due to their limitations in handling large-scale data and providing low-latency access. Instead, organizations should consider distributed storage systems like Apache Hadoop, Apache Cassandra, or cloud-based solutions like Amazon S3 or Google Cloud Storage. These systems provide scalability, fault-tolerance, and high-performance required for real-time analytics.

Furthermore, organizations should leverage data lakes, which act as a centralized repository for storing vast amounts of raw and unprocessed data. Data lakes enable seamless integration of different data sources, provide a single source of truth, and support various analytics tools and frameworks. By utilizing data lakes, organizations can ensure the availability of valuable data for real-time analytics while maintaining data integrity and security.

In conclusion, data collection and storage are critical components of real-time analytics in the realm of big data. Proper data collection techniques, including data streaming technologies, are necessary to gather relevant and up-to-date data. Equally important is the adoption of modern storage systems and data lakes that can efficiently handle large volumes of data and provide low-latency access. By mastering the art of data collection and storage, organizations can unlock the full potential of real-time analytics and gain a competitive edge in the era of big data analytics.

Chapter 3: Real-Time Data Processing and Analysis

Data Ingestion and Streaming Techniques

In today's data-driven world, the ability to extract real-time insights from big data is becoming increasingly important. Organizations across industries are leveraging big data analytics to gain a competitive edge and make data-driven decisions. However, the success of these efforts heavily relies on efficient data ingestion and streaming techniques.

Data ingestion refers to the process of collecting and importing data from various sources into a data storage system. It is the first step in any big data analytics project and lays the foundation for all subsequent analysis. In this subchapter, we will explore the key techniques and best practices involved in data ingestion and streaming.

One of the primary challenges in data ingestion is dealing with the velocity at which data is generated. With the proliferation of IoT devices, social media platforms, and online transactions, data is being generated at an unprecedented rate. Traditional batch processing methods are no longer sufficient to handle this influx of real-time data. As a result, organizations are adopting streaming techniques that allow them to process data in real-time as it is generated.

Streaming techniques involve the continuous processing of data streams, enabling organizations to gain immediate insights and take timely actions. This is particularly crucial in applications such as fraud detection, real-time monitoring, and predictive maintenance. Technologies like Apache Kafka, Apache Flink, and Apache Storm have emerged as popular choices for implementing streaming architectures.

In addition to streaming, data ingestion techniques also involve data integration and transformation. Data integration ensures that data from various sources is combined and standardized, enabling a holistic view of the data. Transformation, on the other hand, involves cleaning and preprocessing the data to ensure its quality and usability in downstream analytics processes.

To successfully implement data ingestion and streaming techniques, organizations must consider factors such as scalability, fault-tolerance, and data security. Scalability ensures that the system can handle increasing data volumes without degradation in performance. Fault-tolerance ensures that the system can recover from failures and continue processing data seamlessly. Data security is critical to protect sensitive information and ensure compliance with data privacy regulations.

In conclusion, data ingestion and streaming techniques are integral to mastering real-time analytics in big data. By leveraging these techniques, organizations can process data as it is generated, gaining valuable insights in real-time. Whether you are a data scientist, a business analyst, or an IT professional, understanding these techniques is essential for harnessing the power of big data analytics. In the following chapters, we will delve deeper into the tools, technologies, and use cases associated with data ingestion and streaming, providing a comprehensive guide for everyone interested in big data analytics.

Processing Real-Time Data

In today's era of big data analytics, the ability to process real-time data has become crucial for organizations across all industries. Real-time data refers to the information that is generated and processed instantly, providing immediate insights and allowing for faster decision-making. This subchapter will delve into the intricacies of processing real-time data, exploring the various techniques, tools, and challenges associated with it.

Real-time data processing involves capturing data as it is generated, analyzing it in real-time, and deriving valuable insights from it. This process requires robust infrastructure, efficient algorithms, and powerful tools that can handle large volumes of data in real-time. With advancements in technology, organizations now have access to a wide range of tools and frameworks tailored for real-time data processing, such as Apache Kafka, Spark Streaming, and Hadoop.

One of the primary challenges in processing real-time data is the sheer velocity and volume of data being generated. Traditional batch processing systems struggle to keep up with the high influx of data, resulting in latency and delays in data analysis. To overcome this challenge, organizations are adopting real-time streaming platforms that can handle data ingestion, processing, and analysis in real-time. These platforms employ distributed computing techniques, parallel processing, and event-driven architectures to ensure fast and efficient data processing.

Furthermore, processing real-time data requires the ability to handle both structured and unstructured data formats. With the proliferation of social media, IoT devices, and sensor networks, a significant portion of real-time data is unstructured. Organizations must leverage techniques like natural language processing (NLP) and sentiment analysis to extract meaningful insights from unstructured data sources. Additionally, data quality and data governance play a crucial role in ensuring the accuracy and reliability of real-time analytics.

Real-time data processing has numerous applications across industries. In the finance sector, it enables fraud detection, real-time risk assessment, and algorithmic trading. In healthcare, real-time data analysis can help monitor patient vitals, detect anomalies, and provide timely interventions. E-commerce companies utilize real-time data to personalize customer experiences, recommend products, and optimize inventory management.

In conclusion, processing real-time data is a critical aspect of big data analytics. It empowers organizations to make informed decisions, detect anomalies, and respond swiftly to emerging trends. By leveraging advanced tools and techniques, organizations can harness the power of real-time data processing to gain a competitive edge in today's data-driven world.

Real-Time Analytics Algorithms and Models

In today's digital age, data is being generated at an unprecedented pace. Organizations across industries are recognizing the immense value hidden within this data and are turning to real-time analytics to gain actionable insights. Real-time analytics allows businesses to make informed decisions promptly, giving them a competitive edge in the market. To effectively harness the power of real-time analytics in big data, one must understand the algorithms and models that drive this process.

Real-time analytics algorithms form the backbone of any real-time analytics system. These algorithms are designed to process data as it is generated, allowing for immediate analysis and response. They enable organizations to detect patterns, identify anomalies, and make predictions in real-time. Some commonly used algorithms in real-time analytics include decision trees, k-means clustering, and support vector machines. Each algorithm has its own strengths and weaknesses, and understanding their nuances is crucial for successful implementation.

Additionally, real-time analytics models play a vital role in transforming raw data into meaningful insights. These models are built using machine learning techniques and are trained to recognize patterns and make predictions based on historical data. Real-time analytics models are continuously updated as new data becomes available, ensuring that the insights generated remain accurate and relevant. Some popular models used in real-time analytics include linear regression, neural networks, and time series forecasting.

However, it is essential to note that real-time analytics algorithms and models are not one-size-fits-all solutions. The choice of algorithms and models depends on the specific objectives and requirements of the organization. Factors such as data volume, velocity, and variety must be considered to determine the most suitable approach. Moreover, the continuous evolution of big data technologies necessitates staying updated with the latest advancements in algorithms and models.

For those venturing into the realm of big data analytics, mastering real-time analytics algorithms and models is crucial. This subchapter aims to provide a comprehensive guide for everyone, regardless of their background or expertise. It will delve into the fundamentals of real-time analytics algorithms and models, explaining key concepts and techniques in an accessible manner. Practical examples and case studies will be included to illustrate the real-world applications of these algorithms and models.

By the end of this subchapter, readers will have a solid understanding of the algorithms and models that power real-time analytics in big data. Armed with this knowledge, they will be equipped to make informed decisions when implementing real-time analytics systems and leverage the full potential of their data. Whether you are a business executive, data scientist, or simply someone interested in the world of big data analytics, this subchapter will serve as your comprehensive guide to mastering real-time analytics algorithms and models.

Real-Time Visualization and Reporting

In the dynamic world of big data analytics, real-time visualization and reporting play a vital role in extracting actionable insights from massive datasets. This subchapter aims to demystify the concepts of real-time visualization and reporting, providing a comprehensive guide accessible to everyone interested in the field of big data analytics.

Real-time visualization refers to the representation of data in a visually compelling and interactive manner, allowing users to explore and understand complex patterns and trends as they occur. By enabling instant data processing and visualization, real-time analytics empowers organizations to make informed decisions promptly, leading to improved operational efficiency and competitive advantage.

The first section of this subchapter dives into the fundamental principles of real-time visualization, highlighting the importance of intuitive and user-friendly interfaces. We discuss various visualization techniques, such as charts, graphs, maps, and dashboards, and explore how they can be effectively employed to convey information in real-time. Additionally, we delve into the significance of responsive design and adaptability across different devices, ensuring that insights are accessible to everyone, regardless of their preferred platform.

Next, we explore the critical role of reporting in real-time analytics. Reporting involves the generation and distribution of insightful summaries and analyses, enabling stakeholders to track key performance indicators (KPIs) and monitor the progress of their business operations. We discuss the different types of reports, such as operational reports, executive dashboards, and ad hoc reports, and provide practical tips for creating visually appealing and impactful reports.

Furthermore, this subchapter addresses the challenges associated with real-time visualization and reporting in the context of big data analytics. We discuss the importance of data quality, data integration, and data governance, emphasizing the need for reliable and accurate data to ensure meaningful visualizations and reports. Additionally, we explore the role of advanced analytics techniques, such as machine learning and predictive modeling, in enhancing real-time visualization and reporting capabilities.

To conclude, this subchapter offers a comprehensive guide to real-time visualization and reporting in the context of big data analytics. By emphasizing the importance of intuitive interfaces, responsive design, and reliable data, we provide valuable insights for everyone interested in harnessing the power of real-time analytics. Whether you are a data scientist, business analyst, or simply curious about the world of big data, this subchapter is a must-read for mastering real-time analytics and unlocking the potential of your data.

Chapter 4: Architectures for Real-Time Analytics in Big Data

Batch Processing vs. Real-Time Processing

In the world of big data analytics, there are two main approaches to data processing: batch processing and real-time processing. Both methods have their merits and are used for different purposes. Understanding the differences between the two is crucial for anyone involved in the field of big data analytics.

Batch processing refers to processing data in large volumes at regular intervals. It involves collecting data over a period of time and then processing it all together as a batch. This approach is commonly used when there is no need for immediate analysis and results can be obtained over a longer time frame. Batch processing is efficient for handling large amounts of data, as it can be processed in parallel and distributed across multiple systems. It is particularly useful for tasks that require complex calculations or extensive data manipulation.

On the other hand, real-time processing focuses on analyzing data as it is generated or received, providing immediate insights and actionable information. This approach is essential when instant responses and immediate decision-making are required. Real-time processing is commonly used in applications such as fraud detection, stock market analysis, and network monitoring. It enables organizations to respond quickly to events or changes, leading to improved operational efficiency and better customer experiences.

Both batch processing and real-time processing have their own advantages and disadvantages. Batch processing is efficient for handling large volumes of data and is generally less resource-intensive. It allows for complex analysis and can be scheduled during off-peak hours to minimize system impact. However, it may not be suitable for time-sensitive applications that require immediate responses.

Real-time processing, on the other hand, provides instant insights and supports real-time decision-making. It is particularly valuable in dynamic environments where quick responses are crucial. However, real-time processing can be more resource-intensive and may require specialized infrastructure to handle data streams in real-time.

In conclusion, the choice between batch processing and real-time processing depends on the specific requirements of the analytics task at hand. Both approaches have their own strengths and weaknesses, and understanding when to use each is essential for mastering real-time analytics in big data. By leveraging the right processing method, organizations can extract valuable insights from their data and gain a competitive edge in the world of big data analytics.

Lambda Architecture

In the world of Big Data Analytics, the Lambda Architecture has emerged as a powerful framework for handling real-time data processing and analytics. This subchapter aims to introduce the concepts and principles behind Lambda Architecture, providing a comprehensive guide for everyone interested in mastering real-time analytics in big data.

The Lambda Architecture is designed to overcome the limitations of traditional batch processing systems by combining both batch and real-time processing approaches. It enables organizations to process and analyze massive volumes of data in real-time, allowing for faster insights and decision-making.

At its core, Lambda Architecture consists of three layers: the batch layer, the speed layer, and the serving layer. The batch layer is responsible for storing and processing large volumes of data in batch mode. It utilizes distributed storage systems like Hadoop Distributed File System (HDFS) and batch processing frameworks like Apache Spark or Apache MapReduce to process and aggregate data over time.

On the other hand, the speed layer is responsible for handling real-time data streams and providing fast, low-latency responses. It leverages stream processing frameworks like Apache Kafka or Apache Flink to handle continuous streams of data and perform real-time analytics. The speed layer provides up-to-date insights that are not yet processed by the batch layer.

Lastly, the serving layer is responsible for combining the results from both the batch and speed layers and presenting them to end-users. It stores the processed data in a way that allows for efficient querying and retrieval. Technologies like Apache HBase or Apache Cassandra are often used to implement the serving layer.

By combining the strengths of both batch and real-time processing, the Lambda Architecture enables organizations to handle both historical and real-time data effectively. This is particularly useful in scenarios where low-latency insights are required, such as fraud detection, anomaly detection, or real-time monitoring.

In conclusion, Lambda Architecture is a powerful framework for mastering real-time analytics in the world of big data. By leveraging the batch layer, speed layer, and serving layer, organizations can process and analyze massive volumes of data in real-time, providing faster insights and enabling better decision-making. Whether you are a data scientist, a software engineer, or a business analyst, understanding Lambda Architecture is essential for unlocking the potential of real-time analytics in big data.

Kappa Architecture

In the world of Big Data Analytics, the need for real-time processing and analytics has become paramount. Traditional batch processing methods are no longer sufficient to handle the ever-increasing volume, variety, and velocity of data that organizations generate. To address this challenge, a new architectural pattern called Kappa Architecture has emerged as a powerful solution.

Kappa Architecture is a modern approach that combines the capabilities of stream processing and batch processing into a unified framework. It was first introduced by Jay Kreps, co-founder of Apache Kafka, to overcome the limitations of the Lambda Architecture and provide a more streamlined and scalable solution for real-time analytics.

The primary concept behind Kappa Architecture is the elimination of the batch layer, which was a key component of the Lambda Architecture. In the Lambda Architecture, data was ingested into both a batch layer and a speed layer, and the results were combined to provide a complete view of the data. However, this introduced complexity and latency issues, as both layers had to be maintained and synchronized.

Kappa Architecture, on the other hand, relies solely on the stream processing layer for both real-time and batch processing. It uses a distributed streaming platform, such as Apache Kafka, to ingest and process data in real-time. This allows for continuous processing of data as it arrives, eliminating the need for storing and processing data in separate batch jobs.

One of the key advantages of Kappa Architecture is its ability to handle infinite streams of data. By relying on a distributed streaming platform, it can scale horizontally to accommodate high data volumes and handle data spikes without compromising performance. This makes it an ideal choice for applications that require real-time analytics, such as fraud detection, recommendation systems, and IoT data processing.

Another advantage of Kappa Architecture is its simplicity. With the elimination of the batch layer, the overall architecture becomes more straightforward and easier to maintain. Developers can focus on building and enhancing the stream processing layer, reducing complexity and enabling faster development cycles.

In conclusion, Kappa Architecture is a powerful solution for real-time analytics in the realm of Big Data. By combining the capabilities of stream processing and eliminating the batch layer, it offers a streamlined and scalable approach to processing and analyzing data in real-time. Whether you are a data scientist, a software engineer, or a business analyst, understanding Kappa Architecture is essential for mastering real-time analytics in the era of Big Data.

Hybrid Architectures for Real-Time Analytics

In the ever-evolving world of big data analytics, real-time analytics has become a critical component for organizations across various industries. The ability to extract valuable insights from data as it is generated has transformed the way businesses operate, enabling them to make data-driven decisions faster than ever before. To achieve real-time analytics, organizations are increasingly turning to hybrid architectures that combine the strengths of both streaming and batch processing technologies.

This subchapter explores the concept of hybrid architectures for real-time analytics, providing a comprehensive guide for everyone interested in leveraging big data analytics. Whether you are a data scientist, business analyst, or IT professional, this chapter will equip you with the knowledge and understanding to harness the power of hybrid architectures effectively.

Hybrid architectures for real-time analytics are designed to address the challenges posed by the volume, velocity, and variety of data in today's big data landscape. By combining both streaming and batch processing, organizations can leverage the strengths of each approach to deliver timely and accurate insights.

The subchapter begins by introducing the fundamental concepts of hybrid architectures, including an overview of streaming and batch processing technologies. It then delves into the benefits of using hybrid architectures, such as increased scalability, improved fault tolerance, and enhanced flexibility.

Next, the subchapter explores various architectural patterns for hybrid real-time analytics, including Lambda architecture, Kappa architecture, and micro-batch processing. Each pattern is explained in detail, accompanied by real-world examples and use cases to provide a practical understanding of their implementation.

Furthermore, the subchapter discusses the challenges and considerations organizations need to address when implementing hybrid architectures. It covers topics such as data ingestion, data storage, data processing, and data visualization, providing insights into best practices and potential pitfalls.

By the end of this subchapter, readers will have a solid understanding of hybrid architectures for real-time analytics and will be equipped with the knowledge to design and implement their own hybrid architectures. Whether you are just starting your journey into big data analytics or seeking to enhance your existing infrastructure, this subchapter will serve as a valuable resource for mastering real-time analytics in the realm of big data.

Chapter 5: Real-Time Analytics Use Cases

Fraud Detection and Prevention

In today's digital age, where the volume of data being generated is increasing at an exponential rate, the need to effectively detect and prevent fraud has become paramount. This subchapter aims to provide a comprehensive understanding of fraud detection and prevention techniques within the context of big data analytics. Whether you are a business professional, a data scientist, or simply someone interested in the field of big data analytics, this subchapter will equip you with the necessary knowledge to tackle fraud head-on.

Fraud can take many forms, ranging from credit card fraud and identity theft to insurance fraud and money laundering. Regardless of the specific type, fraud can result in significant financial losses, damage to reputation, and erosion of customer trust. Big data analytics offers a powerful toolset to combat fraud by leveraging the vast amounts of data available to organizations.

This subchapter begins by laying the foundation of fraud detection and prevention, explaining key concepts and terminologies. It explores the different types of fraud and their impact on businesses and society at large. By understanding the landscape of fraud, readers will be better equipped to identify potential vulnerabilities within their organizations.

Next, the subchapter delves into the role of big data analytics in fraud detection. It explores various techniques and algorithms used to identify patterns, anomalies, and suspicious activities within large datasets. From rule-based systems and machine learning algorithms to complex event processing and social network analysis, readers will gain a comprehensive understanding of the tools available to them.

Furthermore, this subchapter explores the challenges and limitations faced in fraud detection and prevention. It addresses issues such as data quality, privacy concerns, and the need for real-time analytics. By understanding these challenges, readers will be able to develop robust fraud prevention strategies that mitigate risks effectively.

Lastly, this subchapter highlights real-world case studies and success stories where big data analytics has been successfully employed to detect and prevent fraud. These examples provide practical insights and demonstrate the tangible benefits of implementing robust fraud prevention measures.

In conclusion, this subchapter on fraud detection and prevention within the realm of big data analytics is an essential read for anyone interested in combating fraud. By equipping readers with the necessary tools, techniques, and insights, it empowers individuals and organizations to stay one step ahead of fraudsters and protect themselves in an increasingly complex and interconnected world.

Predictive Maintenance

Predictive maintenance is a crucial aspect of big data analytics that has revolutionized the way industries handle maintenance and repairs. It is a proactive approach that leverages data analytics and machine learning to predict when and how equipment failures might occur. By analyzing historical data and real-time sensor readings, businesses can identify patterns and anomalies to prevent costly breakdowns and downtime.

In today's fast-paced and interconnected world, every industry relies heavily on machinery and equipment to keep operations running smoothly. However, unexpected breakdowns can lead to significant financial losses and disruptions in production. Predictive maintenance aims to address this by shifting from reactive to proactive maintenance strategies.

By continuously monitoring the performance of machines and equipment, businesses can collect vast amounts of data that can be analyzed to identify patterns and potential issues. This data includes sensor readings, temperature, vibration, pressure, and other relevant parameters. Advanced analytics algorithms can then process this data to predict when a machine is likely to fail, allowing maintenance teams to take preventive action before a breakdown occurs.

The benefits of predictive maintenance are immense. Firstly, it reduces the risk of unplanned downtime, which directly affects productivity and revenue. By identifying and addressing potential failures ahead of time, businesses can schedule maintenance activities during planned downtime, minimizing disruptions. Additionally, predictive maintenance reduces the cost of repairs and replacements by preventing catastrophic failures that often require extensive repairs or complete replacement of equipment.

Moreover, predictive maintenance enables businesses to optimize their maintenance schedules. Instead of following a fixed schedule or relying on manual inspections, machines are serviced based on their actual condition and performance. This approach not only saves costs by avoiding unnecessary maintenance but also ensures that equipment is always operating at its peak performance, improving overall efficiency and extending its lifespan.

Predictive maintenance is a game-changer in the world of big data analytics. It allows businesses to transform their maintenance strategies from reactive to proactive, saving costs, improving productivity, and minimizing disruptions. By harnessing the power of data analytics and machine learning, organizations across various industries can unlock the potential of predictive maintenance and stay ahead of the competition in this data-driven era.

Real-Time Personalization

In the world of big data analytics, real-time personalization has emerged as a powerful tool that is transforming the way businesses engage with their customers. This subchapter will delve into the concept of real-time personalization, its significance in the realm of big data analytics, and how it is reshaping the way organizations interact with their target audience.

Real-time personalization refers to the ability to dynamically tailor content, recommendations, and experiences to individual users in real-time, based on their behavior, preferences, and past interactions. With the advent of advanced analytics and the availability of vast amounts of data, businesses can now harness this information to deliver highly personalized experiences to their customers.

The significance of real-time personalization in the field of big data analytics cannot be overstated. By leveraging real-time data streams and machine learning algorithms, organizations are able to gain deep insights into customer behavior, preferences, and needs. This enables them to deliver relevant content, product recommendations, and personalized offers at the right time and through the right channels, significantly enhancing customer engagement and satisfaction.

Real-time personalization is revolutionizing various industries, including e-commerce, digital marketing, and online advertising. For instance, e-commerce platforms can now offer personalized product recommendations to users based on their browsing history, purchase patterns, and demographic information. Digital marketers can create highly targeted campaigns by delivering personalized content to specific customer segments. Online advertisers can dynamically optimize their ad placements in real-time based on user preferences and behavior.

The benefits of real-time personalization extend beyond customer engagement and satisfaction. It also allows organizations to improve business outcomes by increasing conversion rates, cross-selling and upselling opportunities, and customer loyalty. By delivering personalized experiences, businesses can better understand their customers' needs and preferences, leading to improved customer retention and higher revenue.

However, implementing real-time personalization is not without its challenges. It requires a robust infrastructure capable of processing and analyzing large volumes of data in real-time. It also requires a deep understanding of customer behavior and preferences, as well as the ability to derive actionable insights from the data.

In conclusion, real-time personalization is a game-changer in the field of big data analytics. Its ability to deliver highly personalized experiences to customers in real-time is transforming the way businesses engage with their target audience. By leveraging advanced analytics and real-time data streams, organizations can gain deep insights into customer behavior, preferences, and needs, leading to improved customer engagement, loyalty, and business outcomes.

Supply Chain Optimization

In today's fast-paced and highly competitive business environment, organizations are constantly striving to enhance their operational efficiency and gain a competitive edge. One critical aspect that plays a pivotal role in achieving these objectives is supply chain optimization. With the advent of big data analytics, organizations now have the tools and techniques to master real-time analytics and revolutionize their supply chain management.

Supply chain optimization involves streamlining and improving the flow of goods, services, and information from the point of origin to the point of consumption. It aims to minimize costs, reduce lead times, improve customer satisfaction, and ultimately enhance profitability. By leveraging big data analytics, organizations can gain deep insights into their supply chain processes, identify bottlenecks, and make data-driven decisions to optimize their operations.

The power of big data analytics lies in its ability to capture, store, process, and analyze vast amounts of data in real-time. By harnessing this potential, organizations can obtain a holistic view of their supply chain, identify patterns, trends, and anomalies, and make accurate predictions. This enables them to proactively respond to changing market dynamics, manage inventory effectively, and ensure timely delivery to customers.

One of the key challenges in supply chain management is demand forecasting. By utilizing big data analytics, organizations can analyze historical sales data, customer behavior, market trends, and external factors to forecast demand accurately. This helps in optimizing inventory levels, reducing stockouts, and minimizing carrying costs.

Another crucial aspect of supply chain optimization is supplier management. By analyzing supplier performance data, organizations can identify reliable and efficient suppliers, negotiate better contracts, and build long-term partnerships. This not only reduces costs but also enhances the overall quality and reliability of the supply chain.

Real-time analytics also enables organizations to track and monitor their supply chain in real-time. By integrating data from various sources such as sensors, RFID tags, and GPS systems, organizations can gain real-time visibility into their supply chain processes. This allows them to detect issues, such as delays or disruptions, and take immediate corrective actions to prevent any adverse impact on their operations.

In conclusion, supply chain optimization is a critical aspect of business success, and big data analytics provides organizations with the tools and capabilities to master it. By leveraging real-time analytics, organizations can gain deep insights into their supply chain processes, enhance efficiency, reduce costs, and deliver superior customer experiences. Whether you are a business executive, a supply chain manager, or a data analyst, mastering real-time analytics in big data is essential for optimizing your supply chain and staying ahead in today's hyper-competitive business landscape.

Chapter 6: Implementing Real-Time Analytics in Big Data

Data Integration and Preprocessing

In the ever-evolving world of Big Data Analytics, data integration and preprocessing play a pivotal role in ensuring accurate and meaningful insights. Whether you are a data scientist, analyst, or simply someone interested in harnessing the power of Big Data, understanding the concepts and techniques of data integration and preprocessing is essential.

Data integration refers to the process of combining data from various sources into a single, unified view. With the explosion of data sources such as social media platforms, IoT devices, and online transactions, integrating these diverse datasets becomes crucial to gain a holistic understanding of the information at hand. By merging data from multiple sources, organizations can uncover hidden patterns, identify trends, and make informed decisions.

However, data integration is not without its challenges. The data may come in different formats, have inconsistencies, or be incompatible with existing systems. This is where data preprocessing comes into play. Preprocessing involves transforming raw data into a format that is suitable for analysis. It includes steps such as data cleaning, normalization, aggregation, and feature selection.

Data cleaning involves removing or fixing errors, outliers, and missing values in the dataset. This ensures that the data is accurate and reliable before further analysis. Normalization, on the other hand, scales the data to a standardized range, eliminating any biases that may arise due to varying units or scales. Aggregation combines data at a higher level, reducing its complexity and enabling easier analysis. Feature selection focuses on identifying the most relevant variables that contribute significantly to the analysis, discarding irrelevant or redundant features.

By effectively integrating and preprocessing data, organizations can unlock the true potential of Big Data Analytics. They can gain insights into customer behavior, optimize business operations, detect fraud, and make data-driven decisions. The insights derived from these processes can drive innovation, increase efficiency, and provide a competitive edge in today's data-driven world.

In conclusion, data integration and preprocessing are essential components of Big Data Analytics. They enable organizations to combine and transform diverse datasets into a cohesive and actionable form. Whether you are a data scientist, analyst, or simply interested in Big Data Analytics, understanding the concepts and techniques of data integration and preprocessing is crucial for harnessing the power of Big Data. So, dive into the world of data integration and preprocessing and unlock the limitless possibilities that Big Data Analytics has to offer.

Building Real-Time Analytics Pipelines

In the era of Big Data, real-time analytics has become an indispensable tool for businesses across various industries. The ability to analyze and derive actionable insights from vast amounts of data in real-time allows organizations to make informed decisions, detect anomalies, and respond promptly to changes in the market. To harness the power of real-time analytics, it is imperative to build robust and efficient pipelines that can handle the velocity, volume, and variety of data.

This subchapter will guide you through the process of building real-time analytics pipelines, providing a comprehensive overview of the key components and best practices involved. Whether you are a data scientist, a software engineer, or a business executive, this guide is tailored to equip everyone with the necessary knowledge and skills to excel in the field of big data analytics.

The first step in building a real-time analytics pipeline is to understand the data sources and determine the desired outcomes. This involves identifying the relevant data streams, such as social media feeds, sensor data, or transaction logs, and defining the specific analytics tasks to be performed. By setting clear objectives, you can design a pipeline that aligns with your business goals and ensures the delivery of actionable insights.

Next, you will delve into the selection of appropriate technologies and tools for each stage of the pipeline. From data ingestion and processing to storage and visualization, there are numerous options available in the big data ecosystem. This guide will provide an overview of popular technologies like Apache Kafka, Apache Spark, and Elasticsearch, helping you make informed decisions based on your specific requirements.

Once you have chosen the components of your pipeline, the focus shifts to the architecture and design considerations. This includes topics such as data partitioning, fault tolerance, and scalability. You will learn about different architectural patterns, such as lambda and kappa architectures, and how to select the most suitable one for your use case.

Furthermore, this subchapter will cover important aspects like data quality, security, and monitoring. Ensuring the accuracy and reliability of real-time analytics requires implementing data validation techniques, encryption, access controls, and proactive monitoring. By addressing these concerns, you can build a robust and secure pipeline that meets the highest standards.

In conclusion, mastering the art of building real-time analytics pipelines is essential for anyone involved in big data analytics. By following the guidelines and best practices outlined in this subchapter, you will be equipped with the knowledge and skills to design, implement, and maintain efficient pipelines that drive data-driven decision-making. Stay ahead of the competition and unlock the full potential of real-time analytics in the world of big data.

Scalability and Performance Considerations

In the world of big data analytics, scalability and performance are two critical factors that can make or break the success of any project. As the volume, variety, and velocity of data continue to grow exponentially, organizations must ensure that their analytics systems can handle the increasing demands and deliver results in a timely manner. This subchapter explores the key considerations for achieving scalability and performance in big data analytics, providing a comprehensive guide for everyone involved in the field.

One of the primary challenges in big data analytics is dealing with massive datasets. Traditional approaches and tools often struggle to process and analyze such vast amounts of information efficiently. Therefore, it is essential to adopt scalable architectures and technologies that can handle the ever-increasing data volumes. This subchapter delves into various scalable architectures, such as distributed systems and parallel processing frameworks, explaining their benefits and potential trade-offs.

Performance is another crucial aspect of big data analytics. Users expect near real-time results, and delays in data processing can have severe consequences for decision-making and business operations. This subchapter delves into techniques for optimizing performance, including data partitioning, indexing, and data compression. It also highlights the importance of hardware considerations, such as storage devices and network bandwidth, in achieving optimal performance.

Furthermore, this subchapter explores the role of data ingestion and processing frameworks, such as Apache Kafka and Apache Spark, in ensuring both scalability and performance. These frameworks provide efficient and fault-tolerant mechanisms for ingesting, processing, and analyzing large volumes of data in real-time. The subchapter offers insights into their capabilities, best practices, and considerations for choosing the right framework for specific use cases.

Lastly, this subchapter addresses the challenges of monitoring and managing the performance of big data analytics systems. It discusses various tools and techniques for monitoring system health, identifying bottlenecks, and optimizing resource utilization. It also emphasizes the importance of performance testing and benchmarking to ensure that analytics systems meet the required performance standards.

Whether you are a data scientist, a data engineer, or a business executive, understanding scalability and performance considerations in big data analytics is paramount. This subchapter aims to provide a comprehensive guide that empowers everyone involved in the field to design, develop, and maintain high-performance and scalable analytics systems. By leveraging the insights and best practices shared in this subchapter, you can unlock the true potential of big data analytics and make informed decisions that drive business success.

Ensuring Data Quality in Real-Time Analytics

In the world of big data analytics, real-time analytics has gained immense popularity due to its ability to provide instant insights and drive faster decision-making processes. However, the success of real-time analytics heavily relies on the quality of data being analyzed. Poor data quality can lead to erroneous conclusions, inaccurate predictions, and unreliable insights. Therefore, it is crucial to prioritize data quality when implementing real-time analytics in big data environments.

Data quality encompasses various aspects such as accuracy, completeness, consistency, and timeliness. To ensure high data quality in real-time analytics, organizations need to adopt a holistic approach that involves both technological and process-oriented strategies. Here are some key considerations to focus on:

1. Data Governance: Establishing a robust data governance framework is fundamental to maintaining data quality. This involves defining data ownership, accountability, and data quality standards. A data stewardship team should be responsible for monitoring and enforcing these standards, ensuring that data is accurate, consistent, and reliable.

2. Data Integration: Real-time analytics often involve processing data from multiple sources. It is crucial to ensure seamless integration and data consistency across these sources. Implementing data integration technologies, such as Extract, Transform, Load (ETL) tools or data integration platforms, can help standardize data formats, eliminate duplicates, and resolve data conflicts.

3. Data Cleansing: Before analyzing data in real-time, it is essential to cleanse the data to remove inaccuracies, errors, and inconsistencies. Data cleansing techniques such as data profiling, data deduplication,

and data validation should be employed to improve data quality. Automated data cleansing tools can expedite this process and minimize human errors.

4. Real-Time Monitoring: Continuous monitoring of data quality in real-time analytics is crucial to identify any issues promptly. Implementing monitoring tools and establishing alerts can help detect anomalies, data discrepancies, or data quality degradation. Regular audits and data quality checks should be conducted to ensure ongoing data accuracy.

5. Metadata Management: Metadata provides essential context and information about the data being analyzed. Implementing a metadata management system enables effective data discovery, lineage tracking, and data quality monitoring. It helps in understanding the data sources, transformations, and data quality metrics associated with real-time analytics.

6. Data Security: Ensuring data security is imperative in real-time analytics. Implementing robust security protocols, encryption techniques, and access controls safeguards data integrity and prevents unauthorized access or data breaches.

By prioritizing data quality in real-time analytics, organizations can derive accurate and reliable insights, leading to better decision-making and improved business outcomes. Remember, data quality is an ongoing process that requires continuous monitoring, improvement, and alignment with changing business requirements. Embracing data quality practices will enhance the effectiveness and reliability of real-time analytics in the realm of big data.

Chapter 7: Real-Time Analytics in Cloud Environments

Cloud Computing and Real-Time Analytics

In today's era of Big Data Analytics, one of the most powerful and transformative technologies is cloud computing. This technology has revolutionized the way organizations handle and analyze vast amounts of data in real-time. In this subchapter, we will explore the synergistic relationship between cloud computing and real-time analytics, and how it can benefit everyone involved in the world of Big Data Analytics.

Cloud computing provides a scalable and flexible infrastructure that enables businesses to store, process, and analyze massive datasets in real-time. It eliminates the need for costly on-premises infrastructure and offers on-demand resources that can be easily scaled up or down to meet the changing needs of data analytics projects. This flexibility makes it accessible to everyone, from small startups to large enterprises.

Real-time analytics, on the other hand, refers to the ability to process and analyze data as it is generated or received, providing immediate insights and actionable information. With the help of cloud computing, organizations can leverage the power of real-time analytics to gain a competitive edge, make data-driven decisions, and quickly respond to changing market trends.

Cloud computing offers various services and tools that facilitate real-time analytics. For instance, cloud-based data warehouses and databases provide high-performance storage and processing capabilities, allowing organizations to handle massive datasets and perform complex analytics tasks in real-time. Additionally, cloud platforms offer powerful data analytics tools, such as machine learning and artificial intelligence frameworks, that enable organizations to extract valuable insights from their data.

The benefits of cloud computing and real-time analytics extend beyond businesses. Researchers, scientists, and government agencies can leverage these technologies to analyze large datasets and make significant advancements in various fields. Healthcare providers can use real-time analytics to monitor patient data, detect anomalies, and deliver personalized treatments. Even individuals can benefit from real-time analytics through personalized recommendations, improved customer experiences, and enhanced decision-making.

In conclusion, cloud computing and real-time analytics are two powerful technologies that have transformed the world of Big Data Analytics. They offer scalability, flexibility, and immediate insights, enabling organizations and individuals to harness the full potential of their data. Whether you are a business owner, a researcher, or simply someone interested in the world of Big Data Analytics, understanding the synergy between cloud computing and real-time analytics is essential for staying ahead in today's data-driven world.

Cloud-Based Big Data Platforms and Services

In today's era of information explosion, the ability to effectively manage and analyze vast amounts of data has become crucial for businesses across all industries. Big Data analytics has emerged as a powerful tool to extract valuable insights and make data-driven decisions, providing a competitive edge to organizations. However, the traditional methods of processing and analyzing Big Data often fall short in terms of scalability, speed, and cost-effectiveness. This is where cloud-based Big Data platforms and services come into play.

Cloud-based Big Data platforms offer a scalable and flexible infrastructure to store, process, and analyze massive volumes of data. By leveraging the power of cloud computing, organizations can overcome the limitations of on-premises solutions and seamlessly scale their Big Data operations. These platforms provide a range of services, including data storage, data processing, data analysis, and data visualization, all accessible through a web-based interface.

One of the key advantages of using cloud-based Big Data platforms is the ability to handle real-time data processing. Traditional batch processing methods often struggle to keep up with the speed at which data is generated in today's connected world. Cloud-based platforms offer real-time processing capabilities, enabling businesses to gain immediate insights and take prompt actions based on the latest data.

Furthermore, cloud-based Big Data platforms eliminate the need for upfront infrastructure investments and maintenance costs. Organizations can leverage the pay-as-you-go model, paying only for the resources and services they use. This makes Big Data analytics more accessible to businesses of all sizes, democratizing the field and allowing even small startups to harness the power of data.

In addition to the platform itself, cloud-based Big Data services provide a wide range of tools and frameworks to simplify the development and deployment of Big Data applications. These services offer pre-built machine learning models, predictive analytics algorithms, and data visualization tools, empowering users with advanced analytics capabilities without requiring specialized skills.

Whether you are a data scientist, a business analyst, or an executive looking to harness the power of Big Data analytics, cloud-based platforms and services offer a comprehensive solution. By eliminating the infrastructure constraints, providing real-time processing capabilities, and offering a suite of advanced tools, these platforms enable organizations to derive valuable insights from their Big Data and drive innovation. Embracing cloud-based Big Data platforms is no longer an option but a necessity for businesses to stay competitive in the era of data-driven decision-making.

Real-Time Analytics as a Service

In today's data-driven world, the ability to extract actionable insights from vast amounts of information is crucial for businesses to stay competitive. This is where real-time analytics comes into play, enabling organizations to make informed decisions and take immediate actions based on up-to-date data. Real-time analytics is the process of analyzing data in real-time or near real-time, providing instant insights that can drive operational efficiency and improve customer experiences.

Real-Time Analytics as a Service (RAaaS) is a game-changer in the field of big data analytics. It allows organizations to leverage the power of real-time analytics without the need for costly infrastructure and expertise. RAaaS providers offer cloud-based platforms that combine cutting-edge technologies, such as streaming data processing, machine learning, and artificial intelligence, to deliver real-time insights to businesses of all sizes.

One of the key benefits of RAaaS is its accessibility. It provides an opportunity for everyone, regardless of their technical expertise, to harness the power of real-time analytics. With just a few clicks, businesses can connect their data sources to the RAaaS platform and start extracting valuable insights in real-time. This opens up a world of possibilities for organizations that lack the resources or skills to implement and maintain an in-house real-time analytics infrastructure.

Another advantage of RAaaS is its scalability. As businesses grow and their data volumes increase, the demand for real-time analytics also grows. RAaaS platforms are designed to handle large amounts of data and can easily scale up or down based on the organization's needs.

This flexibility allows businesses to focus on their core competencies while leaving the complexities of real-time analytics to the RAaaS provider.

Furthermore, RAaaS provides businesses with the ability to react quickly to changing market conditions. By analyzing data in real-time, organizations can detect patterns, trends, and anomalies as they occur, enabling them to make proactive decisions and seize opportunities before their competitors. This agility is crucial in today's fast-paced business environment, where every second counts.

In conclusion, Real-Time Analytics as a Service is a powerful tool for organizations in the realm of big data analytics. It offers accessibility, scalability, and agility, making real-time analytics available to everyone. By leveraging RAaaS, businesses can gain a competitive edge by making data-driven decisions in real-time, driving operational efficiency, and delivering exceptional customer experiences. Whether you are a small startup or a large enterprise, RAaaS is a must-have solution for mastering real-time analytics in the era of big data.

Cost Optimization and Scalability in Cloud-Based Real-Time Analytics

In today's data-driven world, organizations are constantly seeking ways to extract valuable insights from their vast amounts of data in real-time. This has given rise to the field of real-time analytics, where businesses can make informed decisions based on up-to-the-minute information. To achieve this, many companies are turning to cloud-based solutions for their analytics needs, as they offer cost optimization and scalability that traditional on-premises solutions often lack.

Cost optimization is a crucial consideration for any organization, regardless of its size or industry. Cloud-based real-time analytics solutions provide a cost-effective alternative to setting up and maintaining complex on-premises infrastructure. By leveraging the power of the cloud, businesses can avoid the hefty upfront costs associated with hardware and software purchases, as well as the ongoing expenses of maintenance, upgrades, and support. Instead, they can pay for the resources they use on a pay-as-you-go basis, allowing for greater flexibility and financial control.

Furthermore, scalability is a key requirement for big data analytics, as data volumes continue to grow exponentially. Cloud-based solutions excel in this area by offering virtually unlimited scalability. Whether an organization needs to process a few gigabytes or petabytes of data, cloud providers can quickly allocate the necessary resources to handle the workload. This elasticity ensures that businesses can meet their real-time analytics needs without experiencing performance bottlenecks or resource constraints.

Cloud-based real-time analytics also provide additional benefits beyond cost optimization and scalability. They offer the convenience of seamless integration with other cloud services, such as storage, data warehousing, and machine learning. This allows organizations to build end-to-end analytics pipelines, leveraging the power of the cloud ecosystem to streamline data processing and derive valuable insights more efficiently.

For everyone interested in big data analytics, understanding cost optimization and scalability in cloud-based real-time analytics is essential. By embracing cloud solutions, businesses can reduce costs, scale their analytics capabilities effortlessly, and gain a competitive edge by harnessing the power of real-time insights.

In conclusion, this subchapter delves into the importance of cost optimization and scalability in cloud-based real-time analytics. It highlights the advantages of cloud solutions for businesses seeking to leverage big data analytics, regardless of their size or industry. By understanding and implementing these concepts, organizations can unlock the full potential of real-time analytics and drive innovation in today's data-driven world.

Chapter 8: Real-Time Analytics and Machine Learning

Introduction to Machine Learning in Real-Time Analytics

In today's era of data-driven decision making, machine learning has emerged as a powerful tool for extracting valuable insights from vast amounts of data. The field of big data analytics has been revolutionized by machine learning algorithms, enabling organizations to gain a competitive edge by making informed, real-time decisions.

This subchapter will provide an accessible introduction to machine learning in the context of real-time analytics for everyone interested in the field of big data analytics. Whether you are a data scientist, a business analyst, or simply someone curious about the potential of machine learning, this chapter will equip you with the knowledge and understanding to explore its applications in real-time analytics.

Machine learning, at its core, is the science of designing algorithms that can learn patterns from data and make predictions or decisions without being explicitly programmed. Real-time analytics, on the other hand, involves analyzing data as it is generated, enabling organizations to react swiftly to changing trends and make timely decisions.

Throughout this subchapter, we will explore various aspects of machine learning in real-time analytics. We will start by providing an overview of the fundamental concepts and techniques of machine learning, including supervised learning, unsupervised learning, and reinforcement learning.

Next, we will delve into the challenges and considerations specific to real-time analytics. We will discuss the importance of data preprocessing, feature engineering, and model selection in the context of real-time machine learning. Additionally, we will explore techniques for handling streaming data and deploying machine learning models in real-time environments.

Furthermore, we will examine real-world use cases of machine learning in real-time analytics across different industries, such as finance, healthcare, retail, and marketing. These examples will illustrate the practical applications of machine learning in driving business outcomes and gaining a competitive advantage in the era of big data.

By the end of this subchapter, you will have a solid understanding of the fundamentals of machine learning in real-time analytics. You will be equipped with the knowledge to explore further, experiment with different algorithms, and apply machine learning techniques to your own big data analytics projects.

Whether you are a seasoned data scientist or someone new to the field of big data analytics, this subchapter will serve as a comprehensive guide to mastering machine learning in real-time analytics.

Real-Time Machine Learning Algorithms

In the world of big data analytics, real-time processing is becoming increasingly important. The ability to analyze and make decisions on the fly is crucial for businesses to stay competitive and make informed choices. Real-time machine learning algorithms play a vital role in this process, enabling organizations to extract valuable insights and take immediate actions based on the data at hand.

Real-time machine learning algorithms are designed to handle large volumes of data in real-time, making them perfect for applications that require quick decision-making. These algorithms are capable of processing data as it arrives, allowing businesses to react instantaneously to changing conditions or events. By continuously analyzing incoming data and updating their models, real-time machine learning algorithms can adapt to new patterns and make accurate predictions in real-time.

One of the key advantages of real-time machine learning algorithms is their ability to detect anomalies and outliers in data streams. These algorithms can identify unusual patterns or behaviors that deviate from the norm, helping businesses identify potential risks or opportunities in real-time. For example, in the finance industry, real-time machine learning algorithms can detect fraudulent transactions as they occur, saving businesses millions of dollars.

Another application of real-time machine learning algorithms is personalization. By analyzing real-time data from various sources, such as customer interactions, browsing behavior, and social media activity, businesses can deliver personalized recommendations, offers, and experiences to their customers. This level of personalization not only enhances customer satisfaction but also increases conversion rates and customer loyalty.

Real-time machine learning algorithms can also be used for predictive maintenance in industries like manufacturing and transportation. By continuously monitoring equipment sensors and analyzing real-time data, these algorithms can predict when a machine is likely to fail or require maintenance. This proactive approach helps businesses avoid costly breakdowns, reduce downtime, and optimize maintenance schedules.

Overall, real-time machine learning algorithms are a powerful tool in the realm of big data analytics. They enable businesses to process and analyze data in real-time, providing valuable insights and facilitating quick decision-making. Whether it's detecting anomalies, personalizing experiences, or predicting maintenance needs, these algorithms have a wide range of applications across various industries. By mastering real-time analytics and leveraging the capabilities of these algorithms, businesses can gain a competitive edge in the era of big data.

Integration of Real-Time Analytics and Machine Learning

In today's fast-paced digital era, the ability to process and analyze vast amounts of data in real-time has become a game-changer for businesses across various industries. The combination of real-time analytics and machine learning has emerged as a powerful approach to extract valuable insights from big data. This subchapter will delve into the integration of these two technologies, exploring how they can work together to drive innovation and success in the realm of big data analytics.

Real-time analytics refers to the process of analyzing data as it is generated, allowing organizations to make informed decisions and take immediate actions. This approach enables businesses to respond swiftly to changing market conditions, customer preferences, and emerging trends. On the other hand, machine learning involves the use of algorithms and statistical models to enable computers to learn from data and make predictions or take actions without being explicitly programmed. By combining the two, organizations can harness the power of real-time analytics to feed data into machine learning models, empowering them to continuously adapt and improve their predictions and actions.

One of the key benefits of integrating real-time analytics and machine learning is the ability to leverage data streams to continuously train and refine models. Traditional machine learning approaches often rely on static datasets, limiting their ability to adapt to changing conditions. However, by integrating real-time analytics, organizations can feed streaming data to their machine learning models, enabling them to learn and adapt in real-time.

This integration also opens up new possibilities for real-time decision-making and automation. By applying machine learning algorithms to real-time data streams, organizations can make instant predictions and take automated actions, such as personalized recommendations, fraud detection, or dynamic pricing. This not only enhances operational efficiency but also enables businesses to deliver personalized experiences to their customers, resulting in increased customer satisfaction and loyalty.

Furthermore, the integration of real-time analytics and machine learning can uncover hidden patterns and insights in big data. By analyzing data in real-time and continuously updating machine learning models, organizations can gain a deeper understanding of their data, identify trends, and make accurate predictions. This can drive proactive decision-making, allowing organizations to stay ahead of the competition and capitalize on emerging opportunities.

In conclusion, the integration of real-time analytics and machine learning holds immense potential for businesses engaged in big data analytics. By combining the power of analyzing data in real-time with machine learning algorithms, organizations can unlock valuable insights, drive innovation, and make informed decisions. Whether you are a data scientist, a business executive, or a technology enthusiast, understanding the integration of real-time analytics and machine learning is crucial in today's data-driven world. Stay tuned as we explore practical examples and implementation strategies in the upcoming chapters, enabling you to master real-time analytics in big data and unlock its full potential for your organization.

Real-Time Anomaly Detection using Machine Learning

In today's digital era, the amount of data being generated is growing exponentially. The ability to extract meaningful insights from this vast amount of information is becoming increasingly crucial for businesses across all industries. This is where real-time analytics and big data come into play. One of the most important aspects of real-time analytics is anomaly detection, which helps identify abnormal patterns or outliers in data that could indicate potential issues or opportunities.

In this subchapter, we will explore the concept of real-time anomaly detection using machine learning algorithms. Machine learning is a branch of artificial intelligence that enables computers to learn and make predictions or take actions without being explicitly programmed. By harnessing the power of machine learning, businesses can automate the detection of anomalies in real-time, enabling them to respond promptly to critical events.

The subchapter will start by introducing the basics of anomaly detection and its significance in big data analytics. We will delve into different types of anomalies, including point anomalies, contextual anomalies, and collective anomalies, providing real-world examples to help readers grasp the concept more effectively.

Next, we will discuss various machine learning algorithms commonly used for real-time anomaly detection, such as Isolation Forest, One-Class Support Vector Machines, and Autoencoders. Each algorithm will be explained in a simple and easy-to-understand manner, ensuring that even readers without an extensive technical background can follow along.

Furthermore, we will explore the challenges and considerations involved in implementing real-time anomaly detection. This will include topics like data preprocessing, model training, and evaluation, as well as the importance of continuous learning and adaptation to evolving data patterns.

To conclude the subchapter, we will discuss the potential applications and benefits of real-time anomaly detection in different industries, such as finance, cybersecurity, and healthcare. By understanding how real-time anomaly detection can enhance decision-making processes and mitigate risks, readers will gain valuable insights into how they can leverage these techniques in their own organizations.

Overall, this subchapter aims to provide a comprehensive guide to real-time anomaly detection using machine learning for anyone interested in the field of big data analytics. Whether you are a business professional, data scientist, or simply curious about the topic, this subchapter will equip you with the knowledge and tools necessary to leverage real-time analytics and detect anomalies in your data effectively.

Chapter 9: Security and Privacy in Real-Time Analytics

Challenges and Risks in Real-Time Analytics Security

In today's data-driven world, real-time analytics has become an essential tool for businesses in all industries. The ability to process and analyze large volumes of data in real-time provides organizations with valuable insights that can drive decision-making, improve operational efficiency, and enhance customer experiences. However, with the benefits of real-time analytics come significant challenges and risks, especially in terms of security.

One of the biggest challenges in real-time analytics security is the sheer volume and velocity of data being processed. With big data analytics, organizations are constantly collecting and analyzing massive amounts of data from various sources. Ensuring the security of this data throughout the entire analytics process is a complex task. Any vulnerability or breach in the system can lead to unauthorized access, data leakage, or even the compromise of critical business information.

Another challenge lies in the diversity and complexity of data sources. Real-time analytics often involves integrating data from multiple sources, including internal databases, external APIs, and even social media platforms. Each source has its own unique security requirements and potential vulnerabilities. Ensuring that all data sources are secure and properly integrated is crucial to maintain the integrity and accuracy of real-time analytics results.

Furthermore, the speed at which real-time analytics operates poses additional risks. Traditional security measures may not be sufficient to keep up with the rapid pace of data processing, leaving organizations vulnerable to cyber-attacks or data breaches. Real-time security solutions need to be agile and capable of detecting and responding to threats in real-time, without slowing down the analytics process or impacting performance.

Additionally, privacy concerns and compliance regulations add another layer of complexity to real-time analytics security. Organizations must ensure that sensitive data, such as personally identifiable information, is protected and handled in accordance with legal requirements. Failure to comply with regulations can result in severe penalties and reputational damage.

To address these challenges and mitigate risks, organizations need to adopt a comprehensive approach to real-time analytics security. This includes implementing robust security measures at every stage of the analytics process, from data collection and storage to analysis and reporting. It also involves continuous monitoring and proactive threat detection, as well as regular security audits and updates.

In conclusion, while real-time analytics offers immense benefits to organizations in the realm of big data analytics, it also presents significant challenges and risks in terms of security. Understanding and addressing these challenges is crucial for organizations to leverage the power of real-time analytics while safeguarding their data and maintaining their competitive edge in today's data-driven landscape.

Data Privacy and Compliance Considerations

In the digital age, where data is king, securing and protecting sensitive information has become more critical than ever. As the field of big data analytics continues to grow, it is imperative for organizations and individuals alike to understand the importance of data privacy and compliance considerations. This subchapter aims to provide a comprehensive guide for everyone, regardless of their familiarity with big data analytics, on how to navigate the complex landscape of data privacy and compliance.

Data privacy refers to the protection of personal information collected, stored, and processed by organizations. With the increasing amount of data being generated, it is crucial to implement robust security measures to ensure the confidentiality, integrity, and availability of this data. This subchapter will delve into various data privacy regulations and frameworks, such as the General Data Protection Regulation (GDPR) and the California Consumer Privacy Act (CCPA), explaining their requirements and implications for big data analytics.

Compliance considerations encompass legal, ethical, and industry-specific requirements that organizations must adhere to when handling data. Understanding and complying with these regulations is not only a legal obligation but also a way to build trust and maintain a positive reputation with customers. This subchapter will explore the key compliance considerations, such as data minimization, purpose limitation, and data retention, and provide practical guidance on incorporating them into big data analytics processes.

Furthermore, this subchapter will cover the challenges and risks associated with data privacy and compliance, including data breaches, unauthorized access, and data misuse. It will discuss the role of data governance and risk management in mitigating these risks and ensuring ongoing compliance.

Addressing the audience of "EVERY ONE," this subchapter aims to break down complex concepts and terminology related to data privacy and compliance, making it accessible to individuals from various backgrounds. Whether you are a business owner, a data analyst, or simply an individual concerned about your privacy, this subchapter will equip you with the knowledge and tools to navigate the evolving landscape of data privacy and compliance in the realm of big data analytics.

By adopting best practices and staying up-to-date with the latest regulations, organizations can not only protect themselves from legal and financial repercussions but also build a foundation of trust with their customers. Ultimately, data privacy and compliance should be at the forefront of every big data analytics initiative, ensuring the responsible and ethical use of data in the pursuit of innovation and insights.

Real-Time Threat Detection and Mitigation

In today's interconnected world, the importance of real-time threat detection and mitigation cannot be overstated. With the exponential growth of big data and the increasing sophistication of cyber threats, organizations need to be proactive in safeguarding their systems and data. This subchapter explores the vital role of real-time analytics in identifying and addressing potential threats, providing a comprehensive guide for everyone interested in mastering this critical aspect of big data analytics.

Real-time threat detection involves the continuous monitoring of data streams and the immediate identification of any abnormal activities or indicators of compromise. By analyzing large volumes of data in real-time, organizations can quickly detect and respond to potential threats before they cause significant damage. This subchapter delves into the various techniques and tools available for real-time threat detection, including anomaly detection, machine learning algorithms, and behavioral analytics.

One of the key benefits of real-time analytics in threat detection is its ability to detect and respond to emerging threats in near real-time. This is particularly crucial in the age of constantly evolving cyber threats, where traditional security measures are often inadequate. By leveraging big data analytics, organizations can stay one step ahead of cybercriminals and protect their data and systems effectively.

Furthermore, this subchapter highlights the importance of not only detecting threats but also mitigating them promptly. It covers various mitigation strategies, such as dynamic access controls, automated response systems, and incident response planning. By integrating real-time analytics with mitigation measures, organizations can effectively neutralize threats and minimize the potential impact.

The content also emphasizes the role of collaboration and knowledge sharing in real-time threat detection and mitigation. It encourages readers to adopt a proactive approach by actively participating in threat intelligence communities, sharing insights, and staying updated on the latest security trends and best practices.

Lastly, this subchapter stresses the need for continuous monitoring and improvement in real-time threat detection and mitigation strategies. As threats continue to evolve, organizations must constantly adapt and enhance their analytics capabilities to stay ahead. It provides practical tips and recommendations for ongoing improvement, including the use of data visualization, regular audits, and feedback loops.

In conclusion, real-time threat detection and mitigation are critical components of big data analytics. This subchapter equips everyone, regardless of their background or expertise, with the knowledge and tools necessary to understand and master this essential aspect of modern cybersecurity. By embracing real-time analytics, organizations can proactively protect their data, systems, and reputation from the ever-evolving threat landscape.

Best Practices for Securing Real-Time Analytics Systems

In today's data-driven world, real-time analytics systems have become an integral part of businesses in various industries. These systems enable organizations to derive valuable insights from massive amounts of data in real-time, empowering them to make informed decisions quickly. However, with the advent of big data analytics, security concerns have also escalated. It is crucial for every organization, regardless of its size or industry, to implement robust security measures to protect their real-time analytics systems from potential threats and breaches. In this subchapter, we will discuss the best practices for securing real-time analytics systems.

1. Implement a multi-layer security approach: Start by adopting a multi-layered security approach that includes network security, data encryption, authentication mechanisms, and access controls. This approach will ensure that even if one layer is compromised, the other layers continue to protect your system.

2. Regularly update software and patches: Promptly applying software updates and patches is essential to protect your real-time analytics system from known vulnerabilities. Regularly check for updates from your software vendors and ensure that all components of your system are up to date.

3. Implement strong authentication and access controls: Enforce strong password policies and implement two-factor authentication for accessing the real-time analytics system. Restrict access to only authorized personnel and regularly review user privileges to ensure they align with their roles and responsibilities.

4. Encrypt sensitive data: Data encryption is crucial to protect sensitive information from unauthorized access. Encrypt data both at rest and in transit using industry-standard encryption algorithms. Additionally, consider implementing data anonymization techniques to further protect privacy.

5. Monitor and analyze system logs: Establish a robust logging mechanism that captures and analyzes system logs in real-time. Regularly review these logs for any suspicious activities or anomalies that may indicate a security breach. Implement an intrusion detection and prevention system (IDPS) to proactively detect and respond to potential threats.

6. Regularly perform security audits and assessments: Conduct periodic security audits and assessments to identify vulnerabilities and weaknesses in your real-time analytics system. Engage external security experts to conduct penetration testing and vulnerability assessments to ensure a comprehensive evaluation.

7. Educate and train your employees: Human error is often the weakest link in any security system. Provide comprehensive security awareness training to all employees who access the real-time analytics system. Teach them about common security threats, best practices for data protection, and how to identify phishing attempts and social engineering attacks.

By implementing these best practices for securing real-time analytics systems, organizations can ensure the integrity, confidentiality, and availability of their data. Remember, security is an ongoing process, and it requires continuous monitoring, updating, and improvement to stay ahead of evolving threats. Protecting your real-time analytics system is not only essential for your business operations but also for maintaining the trust of your customers and stakeholders in this age of big data analytics.

Chapter 10: Future Trends and Innovations in Real-Time Analytics

Edge Computing and Real-Time Analytics

In today's fast-paced digital world, where data is generated at an unprecedented rate, traditional methods of processing and analyzing data are proving to be inadequate. This is where edge computing and real-time analytics come into play, revolutionizing the way we handle big data analytics.

Edge computing refers to the practice of processing and analyzing data at the edge of the network, closer to where it is generated, rather than sending it to a centralized data center. This approach brings numerous benefits, especially in the context of big data analytics. By moving computation and analytics closer to the data source, edge computing reduces latency and enables real-time analysis of vast amounts of data.

Real-time analytics, on the other hand, focuses on processing and analyzing data in real-time or near real-time, as it is being generated. This approach is crucial in various domains, including finance, healthcare, manufacturing, and IoT, where immediate insights are necessary for decision-making, process optimization, and anomaly detection.

Combining edge computing with real-time analytics creates a powerful framework for extracting valuable insights from big data. By leveraging the computing power at the edge, organizations can process and analyze data in real-time, allowing them to make quick and informed decisions. This is particularly useful in scenarios where real-time response is critical, such as autonomous vehicles, predictive maintenance, and fraud detection.

The integration of edge computing and real-time analytics also addresses the challenges posed by the sheer volume, velocity, and variety of big data. With traditional centralized approaches, the sheer amount of data can overwhelm networks and data centers, leading to bottlenecks and increased latency. By distributing the computing and analytics tasks to the edge, organizations can overcome these challenges and achieve faster and more efficient data processing.

Moreover, edge computing and real-time analytics enable organizations to take advantage of the vast potential of the Internet of Things (IoT). With billions of connected devices generating data constantly, processing and analyzing this data in real-time becomes essential. Edge computing allows for local data processing and analysis, reducing the need for constant communication with cloud-based services and improving overall system performance.

In conclusion, the combination of edge computing and real-time analytics is a game-changer in the field of big data analytics. It empowers organizations to extract valuable insights from data at the edge, enabling real-time decision-making and improving overall system performance. Whether you are a business professional, data scientist, or technology enthusiast, understanding and mastering the concepts of edge computing and real-time analytics is crucial in today's data-driven world.

Artificial Intelligence and Real-Time Analytics

In today's rapidly evolving digital landscape, the implementation of artificial intelligence (AI) and real-time analytics has become crucial for organizations to stay competitive in the field of big data analytics. This subchapter aims to provide a comprehensive understanding of these two cutting-edge technologies, their significance, and the ways they intersect to drive business success.

Artificial intelligence, often referred to as machine intelligence, is the simulation of human intelligence by machines. It encompasses various techniques such as natural language processing, machine learning, and computer vision, enabling computers to perform tasks that typically require human intelligence. With AI, organizations can analyze vast amounts of data and extract valuable insights, enhancing decision-making processes and driving innovation.

Real-time analytics, on the other hand, focuses on processing and analyzing data as it is generated, enabling organizations to make immediate data-driven decisions. This approach is crucial in today's fast-paced business environment, where making timely decisions can significantly impact performance and competitiveness. By leveraging real-time analytics, companies can identify patterns, trends, and anomalies in data streams, enabling them to respond quickly to market changes, customer demands, and emerging opportunities.

The convergence of AI and real-time analytics unlocks a new realm of possibilities for big data analytics. By combining real-time data processing capabilities with AI algorithms, organizations can gain deeper and more accurate insights, enabling them to proactively address business challenges. For instance, AI-powered predictive analytics can anticipate customer behavior, enabling organizations to personalize marketing campaigns, improve customer experiences, and boost sales.

Moreover, AI-driven anomaly detection techniques can identify potential fraud or security breaches in real-time, mitigating risks and safeguarding sensitive data. AI algorithms can also automate repetitive tasks, freeing up human resources to focus on strategic initiatives and innovation.

This subchapter will delve into the various AI techniques used in real-time analytics, including stream mining, deep learning, and reinforcement learning. It will explore real-life use cases where AI and real-time analytics have revolutionized industries such as finance, healthcare, retail, and manufacturing.

Whether you are a data scientist, business analyst, or simply interested in the world of big data analytics, this subchapter will provide you with the necessary knowledge to understand the transformative potential of AI and real-time analytics. By mastering these technologies, you will be equipped to harness the power of big data and drive data-driven decision-making in your organization, ultimately leading to enhanced productivity, efficiency, and competitive advantage.

Internet of Things (IoT) and Real-Time Analytics

The Internet of Things (IoT) has revolutionized the way we interact with the world around us. With an increasing number of devices connected to the internet, the amount of data being generated has grown exponentially. This data holds immense potential for businesses and individuals alike, but harnessing its power requires the use of real-time analytics.

Real-time analytics is the process of analyzing data as it is generated, allowing for immediate insights and actionable intelligence. In the context of IoT, real-time analytics enables organizations to make informed decisions based on up-to-date information. This is crucial in a world where time is of the essence and opportunities can be fleeting.

The combination of IoT and real-time analytics has numerous applications across various industries. For example, in the healthcare sector, IoT devices can monitor patients' vital signs in real-time, alerting healthcare providers if any abnormalities are detected. This enables immediate intervention and improved patient outcomes. Similarly, in manufacturing, IoT sensors can collect data on machine performance, allowing for predictive maintenance and minimizing downtime.

Real-time analytics also has significant implications for businesses. By analyzing customer behavior in real-time, organizations can personalize their marketing efforts and deliver targeted promotions. This not only enhances the customer experience but also increases sales and customer loyalty. Furthermore, real-time analytics can help detect and respond to security threats promptly, protecting sensitive data and preventing potential breaches.

To successfully leverage the power of IoT and real-time analytics, organizations must have the necessary infrastructure and technologies in place. This includes robust data collection mechanisms, scalable storage solutions, and advanced analytics tools. Additionally, data governance and security measures must be implemented to ensure the privacy and integrity of the data being collected.

While IoT and real-time analytics offer immense opportunities, they also present challenges. The sheer volume and velocity of data generated by IoT devices can overwhelm traditional analytics systems. Therefore, organizations must invest in advanced analytics platforms capable of processing and analyzing large amounts of data in real-time.

In conclusion, the combination of IoT and real-time analytics has the potential to transform industries and drive innovation. By harnessing the power of real-time insights, organizations can make faster and more informed decisions, improve operational efficiency, and deliver enhanced customer experiences. However, successfully implementing IoT and real-time analytics requires careful planning, robust infrastructure, and advanced analytics capabilities. Only by mastering these aspects can organizations unlock the full potential of IoT and real-time analytics in the realm of big data analytics.

Predictive Analytics and Real-Time Decision-Making

In today's fast-paced world, data is being generated at an unprecedented rate. Organizations across all industries are collecting vast amounts of data, commonly referred to as Big Data, in order to gain valuable insights and make informed decisions. However, the ability to process and analyze this data in real-time has become a critical factor for success. This is where predictive analytics comes into play, enabling organizations to make proactive decisions based on patterns, trends, and statistical models.

Predictive analytics is the practice of utilizing historical data, statistical algorithms, and machine learning techniques to predict future outcomes. By analyzing patterns and relationships within the data, organizations can make accurate predictions and take immediate action. This is particularly useful in the context of real-time decision-making, where timely and informed decisions are crucial.

Real-time decision-making refers to the ability to make decisions instantaneously, based on up-to-date and relevant data. With the advancements in technology and the availability of real-time data processing tools, organizations can gain insights and act upon them in real-time. This enables them to respond quickly to changing market conditions, customer demands, and emerging opportunities.

The combination of predictive analytics and real-time decision-making presents a powerful tool for organizations in the field of big data analytics. It allows them to leverage data as a strategic asset and gain a competitive edge. By predicting customer behavior, market trends, and potential risks, organizations can optimize their operations, enhance customer experience, and drive business growth.

For instance, in the e-commerce industry, predictive analytics can help in personalizing customer experiences by recommending products based on browsing history, purchase patterns, and preferences. Real-time decision-making, on the other hand, can enable organizations to dynamically adjust pricing, inventory, and promotions based on current demand and competitor analysis. This not only improves customer satisfaction but also increases sales and revenue.

In conclusion, predictive analytics and real-time decision-making are essential components of big data analytics. By leveraging historical data and advanced analytics techniques, organizations can make accurate predictions and take immediate action based on real-time insights. This enables them to optimize operations, enhance customer experiences, and achieve their business goals. Therefore, it is crucial for organizations to embrace these practices in order to stay ahead in the age of big data.

Chapter 11: Conclusion and Next Steps

Recap of Key Concepts

In this subchapter, we will provide a brief recap of the key concepts covered in the previous chapters of "Mastering Real-Time Analytics in Big Data: A Comprehensive Guide for Everyone." Whether you are a beginner or an experienced professional in the field of big data analytics, this recap will help solidify your understanding of the fundamental concepts discussed throughout the book.

First and foremost, we introduced the concept of big data analytics and its significance in today's data-driven world. We discussed how big data analytics involves the collection, processing, and analysis of vast amounts of data to extract valuable insights and make informed decisions. Understanding the importance of big data analytics is crucial for individuals and organizations looking to leverage the power of data in their decision-making processes.

Next, we delved into the various components of a big data analytics ecosystem. We explored the role of data ingestion, storage, processing, and analysis in capturing, storing, and deriving actionable insights from big data. We discussed popular technologies such as Apache Hadoop, Apache Spark, and NoSQL databases, which play a vital role in handling large-scale data processing and analytics.

We also covered the different types of data analytics, including descriptive, diagnostic, predictive, and prescriptive analytics. Each type serves a unique purpose and provides organizations with valuable insights at different stages of decision-making. Understanding these analytics types can help you identify the right approach for your specific business needs.

Furthermore, we discussed real-time analytics and its significance in today's fast-paced business environment. Real-time analytics involves processing and analyzing data as it is generated, enabling businesses to make immediate decisions based on up-to-date information. We explored the challenges and opportunities associated with real-time analytics and discussed various technologies and frameworks that facilitate its implementation.

Lastly, we provided an overview of data visualization and its role in effectively communicating insights derived from big data analytics. We discussed the importance of presenting data in a visually appealing and easily understandable manner to facilitate decision-making and drive action.

By now, you should have a solid understanding of the key concepts surrounding big data analytics. Whether you are an aspiring data scientist, a business executive, or simply someone curious about the field, this book has equipped you with the knowledge and tools to leverage the power of big data analytics in your personal or professional endeavors.

Remember that big data analytics is a continuously evolving field, and staying up-to-date with the latest trends, technologies, and best practices is essential for success. We encourage you to continue exploring and experimenting with the concepts covered in this book, and we hope it serves as a valuable resource throughout your journey in mastering real-time analytics in big data.

Practical Tips for Mastering Real-Time Analytics in Big Data

Real-time analytics in big data have become increasingly important in today's data-driven world. The ability to analyze and make decisions on the fly based on real-time data is crucial for businesses to stay competitive. In this subchapter, we will provide practical tips to help you master real-time analytics in big data, regardless of your background or expertise.

1. Understand the fundamentals: Before diving into real-time analytics, it is essential to have a solid understanding of the basics of big data analytics. Familiarize yourself with concepts such as data ingestion, processing, and visualization. This foundation will help you grasp the complexities of real-time analytics more effectively.

2. Choose the right tools: There are numerous tools available for real-time analytics in big data. Research and evaluate the options to select the one that best suits your needs. Consider factors such as scalability, ease of use, and integration capabilities. Popular tools include Apache Kafka, Apache Flink, and Apache Spark Streaming.

3. Define your objectives: Clearly define your goals and objectives for real-time analytics. Determine the key metrics you want to measure and monitor in real-time. This will help you focus your efforts and ensure that your analytics efforts align with your business objectives.

4. Architect your data pipeline: Designing an efficient and scalable data pipeline is crucial for real-time analytics. Consider factors such as data sources, data ingestion techniques, data storage, and data processing frameworks. Ensure that your pipeline can handle the volume, velocity, and variety of data you expect to process.

5. Implement data quality checks: Real-time analytics heavily rely on accurate and reliable data. Implement data quality checks at various stages of your pipeline to detect and handle anomalies or errors. This will improve the accuracy and trustworthiness of your real-time analytics results.

6. Continuously monitor and optimize: Real-time analytics is an iterative process that requires constant monitoring and optimization. Regularly review your analytics performance, identify bottlenecks, and fine-tune your pipeline. This iterative approach will enable you to continuously improve the quality and speed of your real-time analytics.

7. Embrace machine learning and AI: Machine learning and artificial intelligence techniques can enhance the capabilities of real-time analytics. Explore opportunities to leverage these technologies to gain deeper insights, automate decision-making, and improve the overall efficiency of your analytics process.

In conclusion, mastering real-time analytics in big data is a valuable skill for anyone in the field of big data analytics. By understanding the fundamentals, selecting the right tools, defining objectives, architecting a robust data pipeline, implementing data quality checks, continuously monitoring and optimizing, and embracing machine learning and AI, you can unlock the true power of real-time analytics and make data-driven decisions with confidence.

www.ingramcontent.com/pod-product-compliance
Lightning Source LLC
Chambersburg PA
CBHW052145150726
48002CB00003B/1067